Better Homes and Gardens®
Kitchen Ideas

the AFFORDABLE dream book

WILEY

John Wiley & Sons, Inc.

For general information about our other products and services, please contact our Customer Care Department within the United States at (800) 762-2974, outside the United States at (317) 572-3993 or fax (317) 572-4002.

Wiley also publishes its books in a variety of electronic formats. Some content that appears in print may not be available in electronic books. For more information about Wiley products, visit our web site at www.wiley.com.

ISBN 978-0-470-50894-7

Printed in the United States of America

10 9 8 7 6 5 4 3 2 1

INTRODUCTION

Kitchens demand attention on a regular basis. After all, they function as living-dining-gathering rooms. They're bombarded by heat and water, remain open 24/7, and set the scene for chopping, mixing, broiling, and more. Is it any wonder time takes a toll on their good looks?

If your kitchen is ready for a redo but your budget says stop, here's help. Welcome to the affordable dream source, a collection of kitchens filled with easy-on-the-budget projects, smart style ideas, and bargain-bonus tips.

Interested in what's hot? Run through our top 10 list. It's sure to include some of the items, such as stainless-steel appliances or stone countertops, that top your wish list.

NEED BETTER WORK FLOW? Check out how a freestanding island can solve space and storage problems, both above and below the countertop.

CONFUSED BY OPTIONS? Discover how other homeowners have mixed wood and stone or stainless steel and ceramic tile.

LACKING STORAGE? Explore how shelves can be a smart and affordable solution. Plus they add style in kitchens big or small.

READY FOR A COSMETIC REDO? Learn how the elements of design can change the face of a kitchen.

TRAPPED IN A TOO-SMALL KITCHEN? Sample ideas that add efficiency and elegance to really small spaces.

READY TO REDO? Turn the page to get started.

TABLE OF CONTENTS

kitchen TRENDS

CHAPTER
1

Handsome stone counters and floors, designer sinks, hardworking islands, pantries, and show-off storage lead the list of trends you should know about when planning and shopping for a kitchen makeover. Here are 10 trends to consider.

TRENDS: *islands*

Islands often rank first on a kitchen makeover list. After all, these central countertops add style while serving as landing spots, eating counters, work zones, and more. Size the island to your kitchen, and you'll be navigating kitchen chores with ease.

Give a new island vintage character by wrapping it in recycled wood. Seal the wood with several coats of polyurethane to protect it from additional wear. Or search for a vintage store counter or cabinet that can be adapted for use as an island.

Try the Trend

Ready for an island? Try this trend the easy way: Use a freestanding version—either a new ready-made or an old piece remade by you.

1 If you have only a slice of space and a budget to match, a flea market dresser makes a perfect island. Top the unit with marble or wood, add locking casters, and retrofit with storage features.

2 A rolling cabinet offers multiple functions: a working surface on top and hidden storage for supplies underneath. Equip it as a cart for entertaining that can roll to the party, or outfit it to suit other needs.

3 A purchased island offers the easiest way to bring this trend home. Crisp white paint and baluster legs deliver a cottage feeling; the shelf and drawers make it efficient. Shop for the style that suits you.

TOP LEFT An island is often the center of attention in a kitchen. Give it status with beautiful materials, such as chunky corbels, raised-panel sections, and wood, ceramic tile, or solid-surfacing material for the top. On a budget? Splurge on the countertop and save on the rest of the island.

BOTTOM LEFT A kitchen table adapted as an island adds cottage appeal to a kitchen. If keeping the piece at table height, pull up a stool for working. If the piece is valuable, protect the top with glass cut to fit. Use lower shelves as storage for pretty serving pieces.

ABOVE Think function when you plan a kitchen island. An island can offer storage for bulky items, hanging space for gear, and a top that's handy when multiple cooks join forces. If you already have an island but it's lacking style, remove the cabinet doors and paint the interior a fun color.

TRENDS:
furniture details

Long rows of identical cabinets are out. What's in? Cabinets installed at varying heights and sporting a mix of finishes, fancy hardware, details such as feet and molding, and glass doors or open cupboards.

This elegant island looks like a handcrafted piece of furniture. When investing in furniture details for a kitchen, place them where they make the most impact, such as on an island or a stretch of cabinetry that can be detailed to look like a hutch. Shop home centers for molding and trims that can help you get the look.

Try the Trend

The raw materials used for furniture details can enhance cabinetry whether it's new or old. Search local stores and the Internet to find pieces that fit.

1 Tuck cabinet feet in the toe-kick area; finish the feet to accent the cabinets. Feet come in a range of sizes, woods, and shapes and cost $5 to $18 each. Stretch the budget by slicing feet in half lengthwise.

2 The great cover-up, unfinished beaded board, comes in 4x8-foot sheets for $17 or in bundles of tongue-and-groove strips that cover 14 square feet for about $9. Look for both at a home center.

3 Unfinished brackets come in a variety of styles, sizes, and prices. Most cost between $6 and $20. Add them below cabinets or to accent a counter overhang.

ABOVE Built with scale in mind, this large green cabinet stores a favorite collection. The cabinet looks like the top of a hutch, a strategy that turns this kitchen work center into a dressy space. Note the turned feet cut in half and applied to the toe-kick.

TOP RIGHT This built-in cabinet looks like a vintage stepped-back kitchen cupboard. Feet on the base minimize the toe-kick area while upper glass doors attract attention. Both of these elements can be added to existing cabinetry.

BOTTOM RIGHT Whether custom-made or off-the-rack, wood furniture feet add a decorative base to any style of cabinetry. Choose slender stainless-steel legs for a modern look or turned feet for a country or cottage look.

TRENDS:
open plans

Open kitchens have evolved into spaces designed for living as well as cooking. Making the change can involve removing walls and enlarging openings. Plan for a finished space that feels cozy for one and roomy enough for a crowd.

This industrial-look kitchen is tucked into one end of a large open space but not hidden away. The use of utensil and spice racks calls attention to the working area. A metal-clad island partially separates the kitchen work area from the living room.

Try the Trend

Kitchens open to view need to be furnished as well as the rest of the house. Make careful choices in kitchen equipment and in accessories. Add style with layers of comfort and color.

1 Light fixtures are an important choice. Match the kitchen fixtures to those used throughout the house. Add dimmers so you can lower the lights to set a mood.

2 Washable rugs offer a sound-dampening effect in an open kitchen and add color and pattern. Use runners between cabinets and a room-size rug just beyond the work triangle.

3 Wood armchairs offer comfort and character in a dining space. Use a dramatic shade of paint and a cushion on the seat to showcase your style.

LEFT A new pass-through from the kitchen to the dining room allows better flow between the spaces. Just enough of the backsplash was retained to hide the view of the range. This strategy keeps clutter under cover. In most kitchens, removing the entire wall would eliminate available space for cabinets and appliances.

ABOVE In a small house, removing a wall can make every space feel roomier. That's the case with this kitchen makeover that substituted a countertop-height peninsula for the dividing wall. Selecting cabinetry that looks good for both spaces is the key to a successful project.

TRENDS:
mix of materials

Toss out the old rules. It's time to put together an adventurous new look. Modern hardware might grace traditional cabinets, while maple and oak rest side by side. Painted and stained finishes mix it up.

Painted and stained maple cabinets make this kitchen better by design. Both finishes are highlighted with a darker stain to add the look of age. Shiny black countertops contrast with the white ceramic tile backsplash. Wrought-iron knobs accent the cabinets. A successful mix can be based on color, shape, sheen, or material.

Try the Trend

A dated kitchen is a perfect testing ground for new materials. Gather samples and bring them home for a trial run. Organize around color.

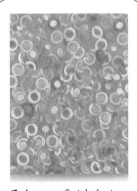

1 A matte-finish design adds fun to laminate countertops. Laminate is an affordable countertop option and pairs well with wood or laminate cabinetry and wood or laminate flooring.

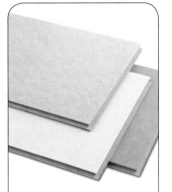

2 Glueless linoleum planks and tiles come in a variety of colors. Use self-adhesive vinyl tiles as a less-expensive option. For a twist, use vinyl tiles in the kitchen and wood flooring in the eating area.

3 A mix of fabrics can soften the crisp edges of a hardworking kitchen. Use fabric for window coverings, to wrap artist's canvases to hang on the wall, and even for room dividers.

LEFT Mixing it up works to create a kitchen that's both familiar and unexpected. The island and upper cabinets are light maple, and the base cabinets are dark-stained maple. Combining colors adds more interest to the room. Surfaces include oak flooring, textured ceramic tile, stainless-steel appliances, frosted-glass pendants, and soft sage paint.

ABOVE Rectangular shapes provide the repetition that holds this design together. Glass and ceramic tiles pave the backsplash, while linoleum tiles cover the floor. Recessed-panel drawers frame simple stainless pulls. When selecting the materials for your kitchen, gather them together to see if you like the group effect.

TRENDS:
show-off storage

Storage is a given in the kitchen. Give yours style and personality with clever ideas. For starters, picture copper pots hanging from iron racks and glass-door cabinets filled with collections.

A kitchen island, dressed up with a marble top, makes room for a row of wine bottles stored properly on their sides. Big baskets on the lower shelf offer hideaway storage for extra supplies. Create this custom look by adding a ready-made wine rack and lidded basket to any kitchen island.

Try the Trend

Open storage works for neatniks only. If clutter builds up on every surface and drawers overflow, consider a pantry with a door that will hide the mess.

1 Off-the-rack shelves and cupboards, added to a standard kitchen, create the look of furniture. This plate rack could be hung above the sink to create a hutch-like appearance.

2 Open shelves are a cook's best friend. They can be hung wherever there's a slice of wall space and filled with the stuff you need at hand. Bonus: they're much cheaper than cabinetry.

3 Purchase furniture for the kitchen that offers storage. It's a stylish way to add function and allows you to showcase your personal style. This narrow cabinet fits neatly along one wall.

TOP LEFT A collector lives here. It shows in open cubbies that wrap the top of the kitchen and in the stacks of shelves that keep everyday dishes and special collections at hand.

BOTTOM LEFT Storage comes in a variety of shapes. In this kitchen, flip-up doors reveal baking supplies, and a roll-down cabinet stores small appliances. A plate rack keeps platters and trays handy for entertaining.

ABOVE Stylish storage improves the look and function of this small kitchen. Note the row of spice containers on a ledge above the range, wood recipe boxes on the countertop, and baskets under the counter for vegetables.

TRENDS:
pantries

Butler's pantries—minus the butler—are back in fashion. You don't need a mansion-size house to have one. Space-sleuthing homeowners carve pantries out of back hallways, broom closets, and unused corners. A pantry also can be housed in a piece of furniture.

One wall in a back entry makes space for a large pantry. Simple shelving stretches from floor to ceiling. The lower shelves, hidden by curtains, store bulk items. Upper shelves hold organized food items and cookbooks.

Try the Trend

Create a pantry by converting an underused closet into storage central. Purchase a metal rack or add shelves that suit the gear you want to store.

1 Maximize the square footage of an existing closet by installing metal shelving. Choose a freestanding unit or screw shelf brackets to the walls. Both options offer storage flexibility.

2 A pantry created from an unfinished piece of furniture handles storage with style. Low-cost accessories— metal bins, glass jars, plastic risers, and wicker baskets—make customization a breeze.

3 Jumbo metal racks like this one hold lots of weight. Load them up with everything from recyclables to kitchen gear. Casters make them easy to move. For a storage suite, line up a row of racks.

MEMORABILIA

TOP LEFT A nook next to the refrigerator creates space for an efficient pantry. Wire racks hung on the back of the door and a rolling-bin unit maximize every inch. For extra style, use pretty storage canisters and baskets.

BOTTOM LEFT When pantry space is limited, stretch it as high as possible. Door units with built-in organizers keep food items handy. Larger items are stored on interior shelves.

ABOVE A narrow back entry space makes perfect sense as a pantry. Open shelves provide easy access to some items, while deeper base cabinets hold less-used items.

TRENDS:
stainless steel

Stainless steel pairs professional style with loads of endurance. Make a statement in the kitchen with professional-looking appliances or add a little shine with stainless-steel shelves, knobs, and a deep sink.

Stainless-steel cabinets and countertops add an industrial look that's tamed by wood upper cabinets. A restaurant-style table creates a handy work-and-eat zone in the center of the room. Look for stainless-steel products in a range of prices. Local stainless-steel fabricators might be the most affordable option for cabinets and countertops.

Try the Trend

Start small with kitchen accessories, such as pulls, storage bins, or stools. Splurge on appliances, islands, and cabinetry.

1 Metal tables on wheels let you move your work surface where you need it. Lightweight pieces are readily available at discount stores. Check restaurant supply stores for more substantial pieces.

2 Countertop appliances, canisters, and accessories, such as this pendent light, offer instant access to a stainless-steel look. If your budget is tight, start small.

3 Replace the biggest energy hog in the kitchen—the refrigerator—with one boasting an Energy Star sticker. It reduces energy usage by at least 15 percent. Check out energystar.gov.

LEFT New appliances in stainless steel can quickly revamp kitchen style. To save thousands, choose a pro-style range rather than a commercial-grade one. Consider a suite of appliances from the same manufacturer to ensure that the stainless steel matches.

ABOVE Restaurant kitchens inspired the look of this unfitted kitchen. The glimmer of stainless steel flows from appliances to open shelving to the center island and stool. Rustic finishes on the cabinetry and accessories warm up the cool metal tones.

TRENDS:
stylish sinks

Cleanup will seem like less of a chore when you start with a stylish sink. It's easier than ever to find one or more to suit your style. Consider what you want—roomy for large pots, elegant and old-fashioned, sleek with a pullout faucet?

Apron-front sinks come in a range of materials, from stainless steel to ceramic to hammered copper like this one. Consider the installation requirements of this type of sink before you make the plunge. Because the sink sits on the base cabinet, the cabinet must be altered during installation.

Try the Trend

Call attention to an existing sink with a dramatic new faucet. If you have a bigger budget, replace the sink itself with a bold and stylish new or used model.

1 Apron-front sinks are popular for cottage or country kitchens. Consider the fit between countertop and sink, as well as the height of the base cabinet, before deciding whether you want to incorporate this look.

2 Shop an architectural salvage store for vintage sinks. This model cost $90, measures a roomy 53×25 inches, and is enamel over cast iron. Before buying a vintage sink, check the finish. Repairs may be costly.

3 A convex edge adds a modern look that mimics the feeling of an old-fashioned sink. Expand your options by visiting home centers and plumbing supply shops to see what's new.

ABOVE An undermount sink can pair with any solid top, such as stone, solid-surfacing material, or wood. The streamlined profile adds a tailored touch, while the finished edge makes it easy to clean up the counter.

TOP RIGHT A vintage sink gains new life with a little refurbishing. Check for options at an architectural salvage shop, antiques store, or flea market. If the sink needs a new finish, get an estimate from a bathtub refinisher before you buy. Purchasing a reproduction sink might be more affordable.

BOTTOM RIGHT Brand-new, but old-fashioned in appeal, this roomy sink is the focus of an unfitted kitchen. A skirt below and mirror tile above add to its romantic look. To create a similar look with a standard sink, remove the cabinet doors and replace with a skirt; add a pretty mirror backsplash.

TRENDS:
stone

Stone continues to grow in popularity due to its beauty and durability. Look for stone to update a kitchen or to give it a sense of luxury. Stone can be used for countertops, flooring, backsplashes, and accessories.

If stone countertops are on your must-have list, save with this strategy: Install stone tiles in a small area, such as an island, and use a less expensive countertop material in the rest of the kitchen.

Try the Trend

Stone is a splurge that can transform an average kitchen. For big effects on a small budget, use it only on an island or use affordable stone tiles.

1 Look for these stone and stone-look materials (top to bottom): ceramic tile with super-thin grout lines, soapstone, honed marble, solid-surfacing material that looks like stone, and fireslate.

2 Choosing materials such as granite and marble involves the choice of polished or honed finish. A honed finish gives a matte effect and provides a bigger contrast with stainless steel.

3 Enhance the impact of stone by stretching it up the backsplash. Pamper the budget by using this technique in only one area of the kitchen.

TOP LEFT Stone countertops with thick edges, like this granite one, add a luxurious look. To get luxury without the cost, consider stone-look laminates or solid-surfacing materials with thick edges.

BOTTOM LEFT To get a granite look for less, purchase 12x12-inch granite tiles and install them with a minimal grout line. This countertop cost $9 a square foot installed by the homeowner. A granite slab countertop can cost $60–$120 or more per square foot.

ABOVE Granite with a bullnose edge dresses up any kitchen. Evaluate the care requirements for stone counters before you purchase. Some stones need to be sealed on a regular basis to prevent stains. Most stones make good landing pads for hot pans.

TRENDS:
going green

Making a commitment to the environment makes sense for the cook. After all, recycling begins in the kitchen. Saving energy does too, by restricting water usage, selecting energy-smart appliances, and using sustainable products.

Building a green kitchen starts with product choices. Add energy efficiency with low-voltage light strips or dimmers and Energy Star appliances. Opt for products made from sustainable woods or recycled materials: knobs and tiles made from recycled glass, and cabinets and floors made from sustainable woods.

Try the Trend

This blossoming trend means lots of new products, from paint to hardware. Revamping old cabinetry with earth-friendly finishes is also a green option.

1 A recycling center with bins for glass, plastic, metal, or paper pulls out of a cabinet. A series of plastic bins in a kitchen closet can provide the same function for less cost.

2 Recycled glass knobs add a punch of color to basic kitchen cabinets. Look for other recycled glass products by typing "recycled glass" into an Internet search engine.

3 All-natural paints have reduced toxins. Look for premixed versions and powdered paints with low or no VOCs (volatile organic compounds). With powdered paint you mix only what you need.

LEFT An environmentally friendly kitchen can be design-friendly, too. Consider double-cellular shades to minimize heat loss or gain and sustainable natural cork for the floor. Paints with zero VOCs come in a vast array of colors.

ABOVE Revamping a vintage piece for use in the kitchen is an affordable and environmentally smart solution. Select nontoxic paints or stains for the makeover.

smart PLANS

CHAPTER

2

Even small changes can affect how well a kitchen works for daily use and for entertaining. Take time to learn the benefits of various working arrangements, and then make the modifications that fit your budget. Improved efficiency might be as simple as adding an island or a freestanding pantry.

BARGAIN BONUS: STACKABLE CHAIRS KEEP EXTRA SEATING EASY TO STORE. USE A FEW DAILY; BRING OUT EXTRAS FOR A PARTY.

WALKTHROUGH WORKHORSE

Smart use of space makes the most of a corridor kitchen with **WORK AREAS THAT HUG OPPOSITE WALLS**. By focusing function in designated areas—one by the sink and the other by the range—**THE ROOM SATISFIES THE NEEDS OF MORE THAN ONE COOK.** The width between counters should be 6 feet or less to keep kitchen chores flowing smoothly.

OPPOSITE A dining area on one side of the kitchen provides overflow space for food preparation and a handy location for casual meals. To coordinate the dining room and kitchen, use the same wall colors.

ABOVE Sliding French doors divide the 9×11-foot kitchen from the family room. The pale tone of the cabinetry makes the room feel larger. In a small galley kitchen, make smart use of the space by providing countertops near each appliance. If the aisle between the counters allows, add a narrow island work surface with 3 feet around all sides for traffic clearance.

TOP RIGHT Sliding barn-door hardware, available through agricultural supply companies, features an exposed overhead track that adds architectural interest. Sliding doors like this fit into tight spots where there's no space for a door to swing.

BOTTOM RIGHT Cabinetry lines a center aisle and stretches to the ceiling to maximize space. Upper cabinets are sacrificed on one side to keep the kitchen from feeling claustrophobic. Open stainless-steel shelving provides some stacking space.

Island Basics

An island can add work and eating space. Here's what to consider before adding one to your kitchen.

- IS THERE SPACE? ALLOW FOR AT LEAST 3 FEET, AND PREFERABLY 4 FEET, TO MANEUVER AROUND ALL SIDES OF THE ISLAND.

- WILL AN ISLAND IMPROVE EFFICIENCY? A LARGE ISLAND CAN INTERFERE WITH TRAFFIC BETWEEN WORK ZONES.

- NEED COUNTERSPACE? A LARGE COUNTERTOP CAN BECOME A LANDING PAD THAT ENCOURAGES CLUTTER.

- WILL A MOVABLE ISLAND WORK BEST? EQUIP AN ISLAND WITH CASTERS SO IT'S EASY TO MOVE TO WHERE YOU WORK.

OPEN FOR BUSINESS

When a small kitchen is hemmed in, **CONSIDER REMOVING ONE WALL TO OPEN UP THE ROOM TO LIGHT AND SPACE**. That's the tactic used here. The homeowners removed the wall dividing the kitchen and dining area and **REPLACED A BANK OF CABINETS WITH A CENTER ISLAND.** Now everyone can talk to the cook.

LEFT Against white walls and cabinetry, black accessories add energy, while the wood floor grounds the scheme. A dramatic black-and-white fabric brings personality to the window. Stainless-steel racks and shelves help the kitchen feel like one a chef might own.

ABOVE A banquette created from cabinet units provides extra seating and storage on one side of the kitchen. Add a table and top the bench with cushions for a comfortable eating nook.

BARGAIN BONUS: PLAIN OLD APPLIANCES? PAINT THEM TO LOOK LIKE STAINLESS STEEL. FOR PAINT PRODUCTS, SEE SOURCES ON PAGE 143.

RING AROUND THE ISLAND

An island works its magic in a roomy kitchen by providing **A LANDING SPOT BETWEEN WORK CENTERS.** It doesn't have to be expensive. This island is made from two standard cabinets dressed up with pre-made table legs and brackets. Outfitted with a butcher-block top, it's a handy work area and a handsome dining space.

OPPOSITE A pretty yellow and green palette, beaded-board paneling, table legs on the island, and an open cabinet give this kitchen cottage attitude. For a really tight budget, paint provides high style at a low cost.

RIGHT Small details, such as the classic bracket under the counter and the practical towel hook, make a big difference in how a kitchen looks and functions.

Bargain Bonus: Track lighting is a smart solution because it can replace a standard ceiling fixture yet offer multiple lights.

If countertops are in good condition, **SAVE THE EXPENSE** of replacing them by choosing **COORDINATING PAINT COLORS** for cabinets and walls.

OPPOSITE A row of tile adds a pretty detail to the beaded-board backsplash. Using a single row of tile is much less expensive than covering the entire backsplash. A new Roman shade dresses up the existing greenhouse window. Affordable laminate countertops and a drop-in sink complete the makeover.

RIGHT Placed in the center of the kitchen, the island serves as a handy landing spot near the refrigerator. The mini-office provides an efficient place for paying bills or planning meals.

BELOW Pullout baskets add a custom touch and provide open storage for stowing potatoes and onions in the new island. To create the look using existing cabinetry, purchase baskets to fit open shelves.

BARGAIN BONUS:
new hardware quickly
updates cabinetry.
choose carefully:
even a $2 difference
per knob adds up in a
kitchen with more
than 20 knobs.

WORKING THE U

A U-shape kitchen makes the most of **A LONG, NARROW SPACE WITH ONE OPEN WALL.** By wrapping cabinetry and work centers around the U, the kitchen is both efficient and roomy. THE RANGE SITS AT THE CENTER OF THE SPACE, where it's handy to the sink and the refrigerator. (See page 41 for the rest of the U.)

OPPOSITE Staggered cabinet heights plus two retrofit aluminum-and-glass doors (one unseen) help plain white cabinets project a trendy attitude. Varying the wall placement makes the kitchen design more interesting.

RIGHT An organizing unit near the sink keeps notepads and pens at hand. Create a similar look with pegboard mounted in a purchased wood frame.

BARGAIN BONUS: FLAT-FRONT DOORS AND BASIC HARDWARE MINIMIZE THE COST OF CABINETRY.

TOP LEFT Slate-look laminate flooring offers the style of stone without a matching price tag. Glueless installation makes this a do-it-yourself project.

BOTTOM LEFT The white finish of the sink matches the cabinets. A designer-look chrome faucet from a big-box store adds affordable flair.

TOP RIGHT Sophisticated glass pendent lights add drama. In a small kitchen, use clear glass lighting to gain brightness without blocking views.

BOTTOM RIGHT For flair, consider using just a few expensive doorknobs. This glass knob adds a fun and colorful accent.

OPPOSITE When paired with white cabinets, white appliances retreat into the background. Eliminating cabinet doors above the refrigerator creates display space. A striped paint treatment adds style, while basic white tiles provide an easy-care backsplash.

BARGAIN BONUS:
need an affordable faucet? check the store brands in home centers for the best values.

KITCHEN GEOGRAPHY

THINK OF THE LAYOUT OF A KITCHEN as a functional map. The position of the appliances, the size of the aisles, and even the shape of the island determine how you navigate. PLAN WELL, and cooking and entertaining will be easy. Learn how A SIMPLE SOLUTION, such as a diagonal island, can make the cook happy.

LEFT A red Roman shade repeats the red used in the glass-tile backsplash. For even more personality, a pierced-metal panel typically used for radiator covers adds sparkle to a cabinet door.

ABOVE Interlocking boxes are another version of kitchen shelving. Before building a piece like this, measure the items you want to display, so they'll fit with ease.

BARGAIN BONUS: NOT SURE ABOUT COLOR? TEST THE EFFECT USING A SMALL AMOUNT IN PAINT, FABRIC, OR ACCESSORIES. ADD MORE IF IT SUITS YOU.

LEFT The back side of the island increases efficiency with shelves for small appliances. Some kitchen designers feel it's safer to place the microwave oven below the countertop rather than in upper cabinets, which can be difficult for an older child or short adult to reach.

BOTTOM LEFT Ribbed glass on the pantry doors disguises the contents. Other products that will create the same effect include fabric panels hung over the doors and vinyl films applied to the glass. Locate vinyl films by using an Internet search engine.

OPPOSITE A standard L-shape kitchen becomes more efficient with a diagonal island that encourages traffic flow. With more space in front of the sink and the cooktop, there's room for family members to work on both long sides of the island. The original L-shape island was too big to work around.

BARGAIN BONUS: TO PLAN THE SIZE OF AN ISLAND, CUT VARIOUS SHAPES AND SIZES OF TOPS FROM CARDBOARD AND TEST-FIT THEM BY PLACING THEM ON A BIG BOX.

MULTITASK KITCHEN

A big kitchen filled with cabinetry can be less user-friendly than **A ROOMY KITCHEN ORGANIZED WITH WORKSTATIONS.** Minimizing the amount of cabinetry leaves **SPACE FOR FUN FEATURES,** such as a **CORNER BENCH** for relaxing and a **BAKING CENTER** that looks like a piece of furniture. Learn how less can be more.

OPPOSITE These 1930s-era glass-front cabinets were worth saving. New base cabinets mimic the style of the original units. Built of affordable paint-grade pine, the units were painted to match. Glazed terra-cotta tiles used as the backsplash were salvaged from the local library. The island serves as a functional room divider because the high side of the island hosts two seating spots and blocks the view of the cooktop.

RIGHT Modern and vintage meet at the sink, where a sleek new faucet is silhouetted against vintage ceramic tile. Mixing vintage and modern pieces gives this kitchen an up-to-date attitude.

BARGAIN BONUS: CONSIDER USING SALVAGE ITEMS AS AFFORDABLE MATERIALS. THEY'RE SURE TO GIVE A NEW KITCHEN VINTAGE SOUL.

LEFT Although the plate rack and baker's table are new, they were much less expensive built by a carpenter than purchased from a furniture store. To save even more, look for pieces like this at a flea market or antiques store. Sweat equity spent sanding and painting will pamper any budget. This center is used for special recipes, so it stands out of the way of everyday kitchen work areas.

BOTTOM LEFT Instead of filling the kitchen with cabinets, the owners struck a compromise between storage and comfort with an L-shape bench. Platters and stockpots reside under the bench top. Thick cushions make this a favorite spot to sit and visit with the cooks.

OPPOSITE These homeowners saved more than $2,000 by building an alcove for a standard refrigerator rather than buying an expensive built-in model. The original wood floor was rescued from under old linoleum flooring. Each savings provides budget money for other improvements.

BARGAIN BONUS: as you're planning kitchen alterations, use masking tape on the floor or walls to mark how changes might affect the floor plan, elevations, and traffic flow.

UNFITTED BEAUTY

An unfitted kitchen is a decidedly European look. MULTIPLE PIECES OF FURNITURE combine to create a KITCHEN THAT LOOKS AS IF IT HAS EVOLVED OVER TIME. Here, the homeowners built a custom UNFITTED LOOK AROUND UNMATCHED HUTCH TOPS and an oversize table that functions as a place to eat or work. An adjoining pantry is a hardworking partner.

◀◀ OPPOSITE Although the kitchen is brand new, it appears to be nestled into an old farmhouse, thanks to lower cabinets that look like dressers and upper cabinets that appear to be three mismatched hutch tops. A two-tone paint treatment on the base cabinets adds vintage appeal. Accessories, such as wicker chairs and a woven cotton rug, soften the room.

LEFT Open to the kitchen, the pantry was painted in stripes before shelving was added. Decorative wrought-iron brackets support rows of shelves. Use shelves like these to hold groceries or tableware, sizing the depth of the shelves to fit the gear you need to store. Lower cabinets offer storage for items that are better hidden from view.

BARGAIN BONUS:
SHOP FLea markets FOR VINTAGE HUTCH TOPS THAT CAN BE ADAPTED as UPPER CUPBOARDS.

Create the look/Paint

① Paint is a perfect makeover ingredient. It's affordable and easy to apply, plus it comes in an endless number of colors. Consider the dramatic effect lime green has on these classic cabinet doors. Light and airy, the color pairs with lavender walls to open the kitchen. Paint the cabinets deep red, and the room turns warm and cozy.

Cabinet Options

Select the type of cabinet that suits the layout of your kitchen. Here are a few ideas to try.

- COMBINE TWO BASE CABINETS AND ADD A BUTCHER-BLOCK TOP TO CREATE A WORKING ISLAND.

- BUILD A TALL STORAGE CABINET FOR A NARROW SPOT BY STACKING UPPER CABINETRY THAT MEASURES ONLY 12 INCHES DEEP.

- CREATE HANDY BASE CABINETS BY SELECTING UNITS WITH DRAWERS. IT'S EASY TO SEE WHAT'S STORED, EVEN IN THE BACK OF THE DRAWERS.

- OPT FOR AN EXTRA-DEEP CABINET TO MAXIMIZE THE SPACE ABOVE A REFRIGERATOR.

- INSTALL A ROW OF CABINET BOXES WITHOUT DOORS. THE OPEN UNITS MAKE FUN DISPLAY CASES FOR PRETTY TABLEWARE.

- USE NARROW UPPER CABINETS TO CREATE A DISPLAY SPACE AT THE END OF AN ISLAND.

- POSITION UPPER CABINETS BETWEEN THE KITCHEN AND DINING ROOM FOR AN INSTANT ROOM DIVIDER. USE GLASS DOORS ON BOTH SIDES TO SHOW OFF COLLECTIONS.

- BOOKEND ROWS OF SHELVES WITH CABINETS TO CREATE A CUSTOM BUILT-IN LOOK.

2 A vibrant color palette pairs with simple cabinetry changes to reform this basic kitchen. Upper cabinets are treated to a striped background using five paint colors against a red backdrop.

3 Concentric rectangles give these standard doors and drawers a designer look. The effect takes time to achieve. Purchase painter's tape in ½- and 1-inch widths. Lay out the pattern using the tape as guides; start taping and painting with the center rectangle. Allow plenty of drying time between coats. For a simpler scheme, use three colors: a center rectangle of mustard, a 1-inch border of brown, and a 2½-inch border of red. Seal all layers of paint with polyurethane.

4 A bright color in a modern space acts almost like a neutral shade. Keep the effect simple by painting the base cabinets and the framework of the upper cabinets in the strong tone. Leave the rest of the space white or stainless steel.

5 With color everywhere, white may seem like a safe rather than stylish choice. White can be perfect though: Use it to brighten a dark room, hide design flaws in old cabinetry, or serve as a background for a bright pop of red painted inside the upper cabinets.

stylish MATERIALS

CHAPTER

3

Every element matters: Fabric and wallpaper give a kitchen texture and style, stainless steel and ceramic tile offer durability, and glass and wood can set the mood. Learn how to combine materials that deliver flair plus function.

SOME ASSEMBLY REQUIRED

Cabinetry is usually one of the **BIGGEST EXPENDITURES OF A KITCHEN REMODELING.** Rather than install expensive semicustom cabinets, **OPT FOR READY-TO-ASSEMBLE (RTA) CABINETRY TO CUT COSTS** without sacrificing style. Homeowners used modern cabinets to update the kitchen in this Victorian house.

OPPOSITE Budget and beauty merge when ready-to-assemble cabinets with a birch veneer are joined by honed Carrara marble countertops in a century-old kitchen. Stainless-steel appliances and cabinet pulls add subtle metal tones.

RIGHT This RTA birch cabinet, a freestanding unit, serves as a handy peninsula. RTA shelves offer stacking storage on the adjacent wall.

BARGAIN BONUS: CHECK IF a HOME CENTER'S CONTRACTOR DISCOUNTS Can Be EXTENDED TO YOU, IF THE STORE OFFERS THEM.

Pendent light fixtures offer **FLEXIBILITY AND UTILITY.** They hang from a socket or a lighting strip, come with adjustable poles to alter the drop, and are available in a wide variety of looks.

RTA or Not?

Buying cabinets off the shelf and assembling them saves money. Here's what to consider.

- KNOW YOUR TASTE. YOU CAN GET A NICE LOOK, BUT LIMITED STYLES AND FINISHES RESTRICT OPTIONS.

- KNOW YOUR LIMITATIONS. MOST RTA CABINETS REQUIRE ONLY BASIC TOOLS, BUT PROPER INSTALLATION IS CRITICAL. IF YOU AREN'T CONFIDENT, HIRE A PROFESSIONAL.

- KNOW WHAT YOU'RE GETTING. VISIT THE SHOWROOM, WHERE YOU CAN ASSESS QUALITY, FUNCTION, AND STYLE. ONCE HOME, OPEN EVERYTHING TO CHECK FOR DAMAGED OR MISSING PARTS.

- KNOW ALL THE COSTS. RTA CABINETS OFTEN REQUIRE IN-PERSON PICKUP, AND OUT-OF-STOCK OR DAMAGED ITEMS COULD REQUIRE MULTIPLE TRIPS. FACTOR IN THE COST OF GAS AND TIME.

OPPOSITE Walls sheathed in white subway tile add a classic look and blend with the clean lines of the cabinetry. Wood tones on cabinets and flooring warm the gleaming white and stainless-steel finishes.

ABOVE A moderately priced gooseneck wallmount faucet lends the sink area a timeless look. Shop home centers for the best prices; look at both kitchen and laundry faucets.

ABOVE RIGHT Use screws and anchors to install brackets for modern shelves. These stainless-steel brackets repeat the tones of the appliances.

MIX WITH STYLE

Stainless steel, wood, stone, wicker, paint, and rugs make **STYLISH DESIGN PARTNERS.** Colors, too, can deliver a fashionable new look. In fact, **PAINT IS THE PERFECT DECORATING ALLY** for updating a kitchen while keeping cabinetry in place. Here's how to pair a warm harvest palette with cool metal and stone.

OPPOSITE Paint in shades of green, gold, and red updates the cabinets in this kitchen. Choose satin or low-gloss paint to reflect light without highlighting imperfections on the cabinetry surfaces. Neutral backsplash tiles let the cabinets be the stars. The ceiling is painted a pale shade of yellow, a trick that reflects warmth in this north-facing room.

RIGHT The new island and narrow pantry fill the room with a warm, golden glow. The island, topped with granite, features cubbyholes for wine and a roomy storage area below. The pantry makes use of a narrow wall space between the windows. The shallow cabinets are the perfect depth for storing food items.

BARGAIN BONUS: COORDINATE BUYING AND DELIVERY. DELIVERY FEES ARE TYPICALLY THE SAME WHETHER YOU HAVE ONE ITEM OR 10 DELIVERED TO YOUR HOME.

OPPOSITE Removing doors above the sink creates easy access to often-used supplies and provides the opportunity to display materials such as wicker, metal, and ceramic. The deep red of the cabinet interiors turns them into handsome showcases. Stainless-steel appliances and satin-nickel hardware add sparkle.

RIGHT Complementary shades of red and green anchor a warm color palette. For all cabinetry, invest in high-quality paint that can withstand daily wear.

BELOW Stainless steel, granite, natural wood, and painted wood create a cohesive materials palette for the kitchen.

BARGAIN BONUS:
ask about a store's policy on matching competitors' prices; then actively shop around so you know local prices.

BARGAIN BONUS: STRETCH THE BUDGET BY PAIRING A FIELD OF PLAIN TILE WITH A SMALL AMOUNT OF ACCENT TILE.

HUMBLE AND HANDSOME

The **CHOICE OF MATERIALS ANNOUNCES THE STYLE** of a kitchen almost as quickly as the color palette and the design of the cabinetry. Here **WROUGHT-IRON BOOKCASES, TERRA-COTTA TILES,** and a **HAND-HAMMERED COPPER RANGE HOOD** create a space with decidedly **SOUTHWESTERN ROOTS.** Selecting materials that establish a regional look you love is a no-fail way to redo a kitchen.

OPPOSITE A hammered copper range hood accented with upholstery tacks provides drama. The backsplash and countertops are paved in terra-cotta tiles. Low in sheen, they complement the painted cabinets. Metal pulls feature reproduction designs.

ABOVE The built-in around the refrigerator offers multipurpose storage and hides ductwork and a sound system. The green-gray hue of the cabinetry softly contrasts with the warm yellow woodtones used in the room.

BARGAIN BONUS: LOOK FOR REWIRED VINTAGE LIGHTING FIXTURES AT FLEA MARKETS OR ONLINE AUCTION SITES.

VINTAGE BY DESIGN

New or old, **EVERY SURFACE IN THIS KITCHEN WORKS IN UNISON**, thanks to a design scheme that embraces a vintage look. The plan started with **AN OLD IRON-AND-MARBLE TABLE.** Flooring painted in shades of gray, painted cabinetry, and wood countertops support the theme. The inevitable **NICKS AND SCRATCHES** will only **ENHANCE THE VINTAGE APPEAL OF THE ROOM.**

OPPOSITE This kitchen is designed for living: The painted floors look even better with scuffs, the wood countertops will mellow with use, and collections will put personality on display. A mellow mix of materials is perfect for a collector. To mimic the look, provide neutral backgrounds so the collections star.

ABOVE The vintage iron-and-marble table is a prized piece that has seen many uses. Here it serves as a kitchen table. Bookcases line one wall with storage and character. Introducing an element like the bookcases makes this kitchen as comfortable as a living room or den. Freestanding bookcases offer flexibility and cost less than built-in models.

BARGAIN BONUS: Keep a running list of needed purchases so you're ready when you find the perfect piece at a bargain price.

MODERN MASTERY

Wood, ceramic tile, laminate, and stainless steel make their way into a multitude of kitchens. Here's how they're used to **DELIVER STYLE WITH A MODERN ATTITUDE.** Consider these examples: **OVALS CUT OUT OF PLYWOOD CABINETS,** wide bands of ceramic tiles installed from counter to ceiling, and solid-surfacing counters on a pivoting peninsula.

OPPOSITE This urban kitchen gains a warm, organic feel from a trio of design elements: oval cutouts in the upper cabinets, extra-wide ceramic wall tiles, and tall stalks of bear grass encased in the resin backsplash. The upper cabinets are faced in walnut veneer with maple interiors. The stock base cabinets repeat the maple of the upper cabinets.

RIGHT Organic shapes, such as these oval cutouts, avoid the boxiness that can overtake a kitchen. When the appliances, standard cabinetry, and windows are considered, a kitchen can become too square.

BARGAIN BONUS: COLLECT PRETTY POTTERY TO DISPLAY AS ARTWORK IN THE KITCHEN. IT'S BOTH PRACTICAL AND FULL OF PERSONALITY.

OPPOSITE This pivoting table sports an organic shape that mimics the oval shapes cut in the upper cabinets. The table can be pivoted into the living room for use as a party bar or swung parallel with the kitchen opening to serve as a room divider.

TOP LEFT The backsplash gets its organic, freeform flavor from bear grass embedded in resin. Superskinny ceramic tiles—2 inches high by 17 inches wide—add modern drama.

BOTTOM LEFT A sleek metal shelf keeps kitchen staples off the counters yet maintains an open feel. Look for streamlined glass containers to match a modern space.

ABOVE Stainless steel adds a contemporary look that suits the design of this kitchen. A narrow border of paint adds splash to the industrial-looking window.

ARTISTRY AT WORK

An existing element in a kitchen, such as a **BRICK WALL,** can be a make-or-break issue. Here's how one resident artist warmed up to the idea of a brick wall and made it **A FOCAL POINT DURING A MODEST MAKEOVER.** Other materials in the space, including ceramic knobs and a vintage table and desk, step in as design details. The final effect is **ECLECTIC AND PERSONAL.**

OPPOSITE Upper cabinetry was raised to allow more space between the countertop and cabinets. New shelves under the cabinets provide open storage for favorite items. Installing white ceramic tile on the backsplash and counters creates a cohesive look. White tiles in standard sizes stretch a budget.

ABOVE An original brick wall is exposed and accompanied by an ornamental window grate. A narrow base cabinet flanks the left side of the range, providing storage for baking sheets. It's the only new cabinet added during the redo. Antique cast-iron trivets and colorful ceramic wall art dish up an eclectic mix.

BARGAIN BONUS: TURN A TABLE INTO AN ISLAND BY COVERING IT WITH STONE CUT TO FIT. LOOK FOR REMNANTS TO SAVE CASH.

OPPOSITE An antique library table, topped by a piece of marble and raised via bun feet, serves as a one-of-a-kind kitchen island. The cabinets are painted a soothing shade of celery green.

ABOVE LEFT With its rich woodtones and authentic character, this freestanding antique secretary contributes to the unfitted look of this kitchen. The dark green-gray tone on the wall provides a pleasing backdrop for the wood and for the muted celery color of the kitchen cabinetry. It also tones down the red tile floor. Early samples of red painted on the walls clashed with the tile floor.

ABOVE RIGHT Handpainted porcelain knobs are a splurge in this redo. Mass-produced knobs in a range of colors can help create a similar look for less.

Create the look/Materials

(1) Shine on surfaces is the common denominator that unites this material mix.
Note the play of light on everything from polished granite and shiny tile
to stainless-steel appliances. Sheen can also modernize a design. To add
reflection, consider high-gloss paints, glass tile, mirror, and stainless steel.

Material Upkeep

Protect your investments with these care tips.

- FOR STAINLESS STEEL, USE WARM WATER, A MILD DETERGENT, AND A CLOTH FOR EVERYDAY CLEANING. REMOVE FINGERPRINTS WITH GLASS CLEANER. REMOVE STAINS OR SCRATCHES USING A STAINLESS-STEEL CLEANER.

- LAMINATE SURFACES CLEAN UP WITH MILD SOAP AND A DAMP CLOTH. FOR LIGHT STAINS, MAKE A PASTE OF BAKING SODA AND A MILD HOUSEHOLD CLEANER. USE A STIFF NYLON BRUSH TO SCRUB THE STAIN; RINSE.

- PAINTED FINISHES REQUIRE GENTLE CLEANERS AND NONABRASIVE CLOTHS. KEEP A SMALL CONTAINER OF PAINT FOR TOUCH-UPS.

- CERAMIC TILE RESISTS STAINS AND CLEANS EASILY. GROUT OFFERS A CHALLENGE. ALWAYS START CLEANING WITH THE LEAST ABRASIVE MATERIAL.

- UNSEALED BUTCHER-BLOCK COUNTERTOPS CLEAN UP WITH A MILD DETERGENT; WIPE DRY. TO DISINFECT THE SURFACE AFTER CUTTING RAW MEAT, WET IT DOWN WITH A DISINFECTANT CLEANER. LET THE CLEANER WORK FOR 10 MINUTES, RINSE, AND ALLOW TO AIR-DRY.

- MOST STONE SURFACES REQUIRE REGULAR SEALING TO PREVENT STAINS. BLOT SPILLS AT ONCE. CHECK WITH YOUR INSTALLER BEFORE TRYING ANYTHING HARSHER THAN MILD SOAP AND WATER.

2 Mixing materials requires attention to detail. In this mix, the grays of the granite are reflected in the chrome faucet and stainless-steel sink, while the blues in the granite show up in a backsplash of 1-inch glass tiles. Note that the colors of the tile vary slightly for a more interesting effect.

3 Vinyl or composite flooring offers high style and low maintenance for kitchen floors. A product such as these individual tiles offers design flexibility as well. Create a random pattern or a traditional checkerboard or plaid. Experiment with the look by dry-laying the tiles.

4 An aged painted finish on the cabinet lends a vintage attitude. To achieve this effect, paint the cabinets with a base coat of a neutral color. Create an antique wash by thinning brown paint with acrylic matte medium. Spread the paint on the doors using a brush; wipe off using a clean rag. Some paint will stay in the ridges and edges of the raised panels.

5 A stainless-steel undermounted sink is set on the diagonal. The new sink works well with the white ceramic tile and eliminates concerns about matching shades of white.

store IN style

Inch by cubic inch, kitchens demand more storage space for a wider variety of items than any other room in the house. Here's how to plan show-off storage for colorful dishes and copper pots and hideaway storage for those items best left under cover.

BARGAIN BONUS:
Free up drawer space with an affordable rack for tongs and spatulas. Hang it above the range.

IN ORDERLY FASHION

Making the leap from cabinet-filled walls to **OPEN SHELVING** might seem drastic in a small kitchen, but it's a move that **DELIVERS MORE ACCESSIBLE STORAGE** and **MAGNIFIES VISUAL SPACE**.

OPPOSITE Tongue-and-groove beaded-board paneling sheathes damaged walls. This product, only ⅜ inch thick, can be painted or stained. For design punch, the paneling here sports a soft apricot shade.

ABOVE Crisp white woodwork sets off the soft paint colors and repeats the sink color. Stainless steel, even if used only in appliances, adds a modern note to a vintage-look kitchen.

Shelves serve as the equivalent of a **FILING SYSTEM FOR KITCHEN GEAR,** while lower cabinets with recessed-panel doors offer hideaway storage for utilitarian supplies.

OPPOSITE Cabinets with glass doors keep dust away and pair well with open shelving. In a small kitchen, shelves and glass cabinet doors expand visual space.

ABOVE To keep the countertop free of clutter, a microwave oven hangs from upper cabinetry, and narrow wall shelves hold jars of spices.

TOP RIGHT Brackets cut in a gentle curve provide support for the shelves. These custom brackets reflect both modern and classic attitudes.

BOTTOM RIGHT Narrow L-shape shelves for spices are easy to install; they add style as well as function. Spice identification labels are on the bottom of the jars.

OPEN-MINDED STORAGE

Kitchen makeovers require **COMPROMISE AND CREATIVITY.** Removing upper cabinetry can **MAKE A KITCHEN FEEL BIGGER,** but the loss of cabinet space can present problems. This kitchen makeover includes a new island that replaces upper cabinets with undercounter storage.

OPPOSITE Thinking about replacing upper cabinets with open shelves? Assess your storage needs before grabbing the crowbar. If your cabinets are filled with dishes that would look good on display, your kitchen might be a candidate for shelves. If your cabinets are cluttered, leave the doors in place.

RIGHT Classic cottage cabinetry with beaded-board panels gives this kitchen a homey appeal. Other cottage materials include tin panels on the range hood and backsplash and curved shelf brackets. A color scheme of pale yellow and dusty blue softens and soothes.

BARGAIN BONUS: TO create an open look WITHOUT SACRIFICING THE BUDGET, remove a few cabinet doors and paint THE CABINET INTERIORS a focal-point color.

Open kitchen storage can introduce clutter. To **SIMPLIFY THE LOOK** of shelves and glass-door cabinets, stack them with gear that blends with shelf, cabinet, and wall colors.

LEFT In a kitchen with stainless-steel appliances, open shelves filled with metal pots and pans fit right in. Use baskets on shelves to create storage that's accessible without introducing clutter.

ABOVE Removing a wall between the kitchen and dining room makes space for a large island that offers open and closed storage. Maximizing shelves in the island organizes tasks. Simple elements, such as a towel bar and metal utensil holders, add accessible storage.

OPPOSITE One end of an island makes a perfect location for a cookbook collection. The books are out of the way, yet handy for use. Keep a stool nearby so the cook can sit and dream up a weekend dinner.

BARGAIN BONUS: CONSIDER TIN-LOOK CEILING PANELS TO COVER A DATED CERAMIC TILE BACKSPLASH. LOOK FOR 2X2-FOOT EMBOSSED PLASTIC SQUARES AT HOME CENTERS FOR $10 TO $24 each.

Create the look/Special storage

① This kitchen balances open and closed storage to suit the cook's needs. Some cooks might want everything in view, just as in a professional kitchen; others might want some things hidden from view to create a sleek appearance. Most cooks want a little of both.

Undercover Storage

Cabinets and handy drawers outfitted for organization effortlessly stow the gear and supplies that keep a kitchen working. Here's what to know.

- TAKE MEASUREMENTS OF WHAT YOU WANT TO STORE BEFORE YOU SHOP FOR ORGANIZATIONAL GEAR. YOU MIGHT FIND THAT SELDOM-USED ROASTERS OR STOCKPOTS ARE BETTER STORED IN ANOTHER PART OF THE HOUSE.

- FOR BETTER ACCESS TO UPPER CABINETRY, CONSIDER MOUNTING THE DOORS ON HARDWARE THAT LETS YOU SWING THEM OPEN, OUT OF THE WAY.

- THE INSIDE OF DOORS CAN BE VALUABLE STORAGE SPACE. INSTALL RACKS AND HOOKS TO PUT THESE SPACES TO WORK.

- FOR EASIER ACCESS TO DEEP LOWER CABINETRY, CONSIDER REMOVING THE DOORS AND OUTFITTING THE SHELVES WITH PULLOUT WICKER BASKETS. THIS STRATEGY OFFERS A STYLE BONUS.

- CUSTOMIZE DEEP DRAWERS WITH DOUBLE-DECKER CUTLERY TRAYS, AND ADD PARTITIONS SO TALL ITEMS STAY UPRIGHT WHEN THE DRAWER IS PULLED OUT. PAINT THE INSIDE OF DRAWERS TO ADD AN UNEXPECTED SHOT OF A FAVORITE COLOR.

2 In a stretch of cabinets, shelves outfitted with baskets provide a happy compromise between open and closed storage. Baskets offer the same function as closed cabinetry, with one advantage: They can be moved right where their contents are needed.

3 Roll up the garage door for service and cover everything up when the job is done. An appliance garage also should include an electrical outlet. These storage features gobble up lots of counterspace, so consider installing one in an unused corner of the countertop.

4 Upper cabinets are shallow at 12 inches deep, so nothing gets lost in the back of the space. Since they also can be too small to hold oversize dinner plates, save them for glassware, bowls, and salad plates.

5 Roll-out shelves inside cabinets make heavy gear more accessible. To retrofit existing kitchen cabinets, look for vinyl-coated or stainless-steel racks.

BARGAIN BONUS: FOR an affordable island, add locking casters to a small table to raise it to working height.

DESIGNED TO STORE

When a designer updates a kitchen, **STYLE AND UTILITY** become happy companions. In this sunny space, there's open storage to add **CHARMING VIEWS** and enough closed storage to **CONCEAL CLUTTER.** The best part is that small changes—removing cabinet doors, hanging gear, and painting—make the difference.

OPPOSITE White-painted antique shelves display part of a dishware collection. Stacking the plates, platters, and bowls creates a sculptural effect; keeping them in view encourages regular use.

ABOVE LEFT Beaded-board panels sheathe the side of the island and add cottage appeal. The antique English peg rack provides handy storage for kitchen towels or canvas bags.

ABOVE RIGHT A corner cabinet, painted soft yellow, becomes a pretty display niche for a collection of white gear. The display focuses attention on a few large pieces for maximum impact.

A **FREESTANDING PIECE OF FURNITURE** can be an affordable storage solution. Consider nestling an **OCCASIONAL TABLE** near an island to serve as a drink center, or put a **DRESSER** to use as a sideboard in an eating area.

ABOVE A collection of platters and pitchers provides functional flair. The pitchers earn their keep holding flatware, while platters serve as handy trays.

LEFT Cabinetry keeps most kitchen gear out of sight, but pretty storage details attract the most attention. Consider these smart ideas: Store plates by leaning them against the backsplash. Keep bottles of wine stored within view. Find an antique rack to use for kitchen towels.

OPPOSITE Freestanding pieces can introduce storage with character. This workbench with a butcher-block top serves as a casual dining space and provides roomy storage for oversize pots and pans. Equipped with wheels, it can move to wherever it's needed.

BARGAIN BONUS: an island stands apart, so it can wear a different finish than the other cabinets. Brush on a complementary paint or stain.

CUTTING CLUTTER

VINTAGE CABINETS provide the style starting point for this kitchen redo. The CLEVER MIX OF OPEN AND CLOSED STORAGE makes a place for everything. High ceilings allow storage to stretch above the height of standard cabinetry, a SMART STRATEGY FOR STORING seldom-used items.

OPPOSITE Wise use of space translates into storage where it's needed. Fitting a smaller range into an existing appliance slot made room for a stack of baskets.

ABOVE LEFT For storage flexibility, equip open cabinets with movable shelves. Add style flexibility by painting the units a neutral shade, inside and out.

ABOVE RIGHT Before building a shelf unit like this one, shop for baskets. The basket size will determine the width and depth of the unit you build.

BARGAIN BONUS: small affordable details, such as a new faucet or knobs, can have a big impact on kitchen style.

A **RADIATOR MIGHT SEEM LIKE AN OBSTACLE** when redoing a kitchen. Instead, think of a low unit as a chance to create a **PRETTY BENCH**; consider a tall radiator as the basis for a **SIDEBOARD.**

◀◀ **OPPOSITE** Handcrafted cabinets original to the kitchen inspired the makeover. The cabinets were dressed up with crown molding and a fresh coat of white paint. When reworking old cabinets, add details such as knobs and pulls that support the vintage look.

◀ **LEFT** A simple bench skirts a radiator with style. If your kitchen has room, consider adding a bench with storage underneath. Options include box bases with lift-up lids or bookcase-style cubbies under the bench top.

▼ **BELOW** Any surface can be put to work. Even the top of the refrigerator offers enough room for handsome baskets. A painted finish and a chalkboard on the fridge front lend a personal note.

BARGAIN BONUS:
PURCHASE COUNTERTOPS, FLOORING, and APPLIANCES IN NEUTRALS SO THEY CAN STAY PUT EVEN WHEN YOU FALL IN LOVE WITH a new wall color.

Create the look/Shelves

(1) Open shelves filled with pretty tableware keep a hardworking kitchen from seeming too utilitarian. Keep the look simple by storing items in a limited range of neutrals; make it splashy with colorful groupings.

Shelf Know-How

A wall of kitchen shelves that stretches from side to side or countertop to ceiling adds drama and provides a showcase for classic kitchen gear. Here's what to consider.

- LOOK FOR PREFINISHED SHELVES AND BRACKETS, AND ALSO CONSIDER PAINTING THEM TO FIT A COLOR SCHEME. SHELVES OFTEN COME IN 4-, 5-, AND 6-FOOT LENGTHS AND IN DEPTHS FROM 8 TO 12 INCHES. CUSTOM SHELVES CAN BE MADE TO ANY LENGTH OR WIDTH.

- CHECK THAT SHELVES ARE DEEP ENOUGH TO HOLD THE GEAR YOU WANT TO STORE. OVERSIZE DINNER PLATES MIGHT REQUIRE AN EXTRA-DEEP SHELF.

- ANCHOR SHELVES INTO WALL STUDS TO SUPPORT POUNDS OF KITCHEN GEAR. ASK FOR ADVICE AT YOUR LOCAL HOME CENTER.

- TO AVOID DUST BUILDUP, LIMIT THE CONTENTS OF OPEN SHELVING TO ITEMS THAT ARE USED WEEKLY.

- GROUP LIKE ITEMS FOR A TIDY VIEW; STORE ODDS AND ENDS BEHIND CLOSED CABINET DOORS.

2 Brackets come in a variety of styles, from ornate Victorian models to plain wood triangles. Choose a style that fits the look you want in your kitchen.

3 An open storage cabinet features spillguards on the shelves.

4 Narrow shelves make smart use of space. Look for shelves that measure 4 to 6 inches deep, just enough space for a collection of storage jars.

5 Add a surprise with a shelf that tops a window and includes a coated wire rack for wine glasses.

decorator TOUCHES

CHAPTER

5

Once strictly utilitarian, kitchens are now treated to the same decorator touches as every other room in the house. Learn how to introduce color and fabrics, incorporate collections, and add personal touches to these heart-of-the-home spaces.

WARMING TRENDS

PAINT AND FABRIC TEAM UP to give a dated kitchen an upbeat attitude. These decorating materials offer a host of options at an affordable cost. Use them to turn an island into a focal point, **TO SOFTEN A WINDOW,** or to skirt a sink. It's the easiest way to turn a has-been kitchen into the **BEST-DRESSED ROOM IN THE HOUSE.**

OPPOSITE A couple of yards of playful floral-print fabric (on window shade, pendent shade, and pillow) inspired the color palette. Removing upper cabinet doors and painting interiors adds even more color.

ABOVE Striping the backsplash with alternating broad red bands and thin olive stripes on white gives the kitchen bold scale, uniting the intricate fabric pattern and the red island.

BARGAIN BONUS: BUY SAMPLE POTS OF PAINT OR CRAFTS PAINT FOR ADDING SMALL DETAILS, SUCH AS A STENCIL OR A STRIPE ON THE BACKSPLASH.

If you love your stained wood cabinets but **CRAVE COLOR,** follow this strategy. Select a fabric first; then **MATCH PAINT COLORS TO THE FABRIC** and use them on an island or backsplash.

TOP LEFT Here's one smart way to make an island. Start with two unfinished dressers, trim their legs to counter height, and screw them together back-to-back beneath a white-stained solid-core door. The stencil adds flair.

TOP RIGHT White stain freshens an unfinished stool. The skirted seat cushion and pillow add comfort. On the seat cushion, grommets and ties secure the cover.

BOTTOM LEFT This simple-to-make window shade starts with a length of fabric. Fold and fuse the sides and bottom of the shade to fit the window opening; stitch a casing for a tension rod on the top edge. Tack two sets of ties to the shade top; tie them to gather the shade to length.

BOTTOM RIGHT To minimize a long block of cabinetry, remove the doors below the sink and replace with a fabric skirt. The skirt is mounted to the cabinet frame with hook-and-loop tape. Glass buttons embellish the skirt pleats.

OPPOSITE To cover a lampshade with fabric, spray both the shade and the fabric back with spray adhesive. Wrap the shade in fabric, tuck the fabric edges to the inside of the shade—top and bottom—and secure with fabric glue. Avoid stripes and other linear patterns when covering an angled lampshade.

BARGAIN BONUS: SEARCH FOR AFFORDABLE FABRICS AT FABRIC OUTLET STORES. CHECK THE YELLOW PAGES. ALSO SIGN UP FOR EMAIL SALES ALERTS FROM LOCAL FABRIC STORES.

SCANDINAVIAN AT HEART

A cool white palette plus new and old metals add Nordic flair to this kitchen. **WORK AND STORAGE STATIONS** spread around the room deliver **RESTAURANT-STYLE EFFICIENCY.** This strategy works especially well in a kitchen with walls broken up by multiple doorways and with **ODDLY SHAPED NOOKS TO FILL.** White paint becomes the affordable unifier.

OPPOSITE A one-of-a-kind antique bakery table serves as the focal point of the space. Look for other pieces—a farm table, roomy dresser, or rustic workbench—to transform into kitchen storage and workspace. Add casters to raise the piece up to 36 inches high for comfortable working height.

RIGHT A long wall provides storage options. Open shelves, a skirted counter, and a pantry behind French doors make room for everything from glassware to well-used pots and pans.

BARGAIN BONUS: SUBSTITUTE INEXPENSIVE FABRIC SKIRTS FOR LOWER CABINETRY DOORS. BUY A LENGTH OF FABRIC AND HANG IT FROM A TENSION ROD.

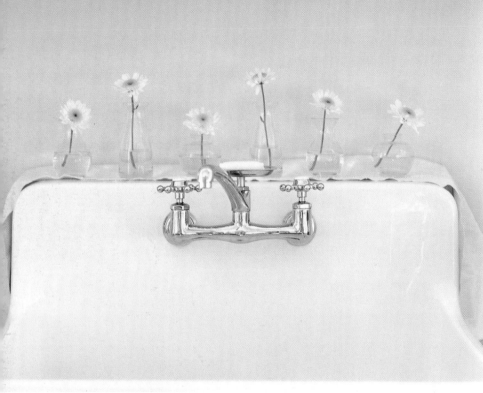

LEFT Beef up open shelves with doubled-up brackets and chunky crown molding applied around the perimeter.

ABOVE The shelf above the sink features cubbyholes that keep dinnerware organized and ready for setting the table.

TOP RIGHT Painted furniture and floorings, Roman shades, and storage baskets create a Scandinavian look in the kitchen eating area. A fitted slipcover on the table pops into the wash.

BOTTOM RIGHT A rolling storage bin nestles under shelves at one end of the room. Built of plywood, the bin has compartments sized to hold pantry supplies; casters let it roll where it's needed.

BARGAIN BONUS: make your own shade of white paint. Buy cheap "as is" cans of paint in white and off-white shades; mix them in a 5-gallon paint bucket.

ABOVE LEFT To create a designer look in your kitchen, copy these ideas: Hang a crystal-trimmed chandelier, gather supplies in handsome glass canisters, and skirt a chair.

ABOVE RIGHT Fabric panels hide the pantry without taking away from the open feel of French doors. For door curtains, use rods that screw to the backs of the doors. Shelves inside the pantry can be moved as needed for storing large items.

PLAYING WITH COLOR

A **NEUTRAL KITCHEN** is a safe choice, but it can get boring. The strategy used in this kitchen—**ADDING COLORFUL ACCESSORIES AND FURNITURE**—is a perfect fit if your budget is tight or if you like to change your mind. Start by **PLAYING WITH COLOR**. Try various combinations, **CHANGE HUES WITH EACH SEASON**, and learn what works.

OPPOSITE Pops of island color are all the decorating that's needed in a kitchen with a cottage attitude. The pure white backdrop offers perfect color contrast. Simple cafe curtains provide privacy.

TOP RIGHT Open cabinetry lets everyday dishes function as eye-popping art. Even the spatulas, grouped in a pitcher, help brighten the room. Using colorful accessories is a no-commitment strategy for adding bright hues to a white kitchen. Note the mood-lifting effect of painting French doors aqua blue.

BOTTOM RIGHT A string stretched from cabinet to cabinet above the sink provides a charming way to display a collection of napkins. This toss-and-go idea is super easy. For even more color, prop a plate in each window.

BARGAIN BONUS: napkins are an affordable option for introducing colorful fabric. Use them as window treatments or chair slipcovers.

GOING DRESSY

In a house without a formal dining room, **THE KITCHEN HAS TO DRESS UP** for entertaining and still be efficient for every day. That means **PAINTING CABINETRY** to match the walls, using stylish **BLACK GRANITE FOR COUNTERTOPS**, adding **OPEN SHELVES** to hold collections, **DRAPING CURTAINS** from floor to ceiling, and **HANGING AN ORNATE MIRROR** to reflect the view.

OPPOSITE A dressed-up dining table and freestanding refrigerator are happy companions in this kitchen. A classic color scheme, dressy details such as a gilt mirror, and an elegant granite countertop perfect the look.

ABOVE Open shelves above the range provide a staging area for collectibles that can be used for entertaining. The shelves, edged in molding and held up by graceful brackets, mimic the look of a handsome hutch.

BARGAIN BONUS: LIGHT a countertop WITH inexpensive DESK LAMPS RATHER THAN PAYING an ELECTRICIAN TO INSTALL undercabinet LIGHTING.

BARGAIN BONUS: CREATE an INEXPENSIVE PENDENT BY HANGING an ALUMINUM WORK LIGHT AND PLUGGING IT INTO an OUTLET.

OPPOSITE Painting kitchen cabinetry the same color as the walls helps the working zones of the kitchen blend into the background. The dressy French chair and ornate mirror provide contrast with the wall of cabinetry.

TOP LEFT The kitchen dining area is dressy enough for company—perfect for a home that lacks a formal dining space. Leaves expand the table to cozily seat up to 10. A Victorian cabinet and curtains made of polished cotton add decorator touches.

BOTTOM LEFT Collections fill silverplate bowls on the shelves, adding fun and personality to a hardworking room.

ABOVE Classic materials—honed granite and subway tile—add a style splash. Get maximum effect on a budget by using the granite only on a small stretch of countertop. Subway tile is an affordable material, especially if you can install the product yourself. Look for instructions for installing tile at bhg.com.

BUNGALOW REBORN

A GOOD KITCHEN CAN BE MADE BETTER. Consider the net effect of replacing a few cabinets with OPEN SHELVES, beefing up MOLDINGS, introducing a NEUTRAL PALETTE, splurging for AN APRON-FRONT SINK, and replacing old counters with HANDSOME WOOD ONES.

OPPOSITE New shelves take the place of upper cabinets and deliver style along with easy access to tableware. The apron-front sink sets the tone for this bungalow kitchen, while a khaki and cream palette unifies the space.

ABOVE Refine the look of base cabinets by covering the dishwasher with a cabinet look-alike. Start with a dishwasher that has a top control panel and an extra-slim face to accept a false-front panel that matches the cabinetry.

BARGAIN BONUS: SHOP FOR NEW APPLIANCES WHEN THE MARKET IS SLOW, SUCH AS DURING THE MONTH OF DECEMBER.

Consider a **SOPHISTICATED COLOR PALETTE** of warm or cool neutrals as a background that can freshen and **DISGUISE UNUSUAL CABINET CONFIGURATIONS** or worn cabinets.

OPPOSITE Pot storage above the range keeps equipment handy. Consider using decorative lamps on the countertop to add a soft glow while dinner is served.

ABOVE LEFT Free up counterspace by placing the microwave oven below the counter. This step might require a little carpentry, but it's worth the expense. Beaded board stretches along the backsplash and up to the crown molding that wraps the room at cabinet height.

ABOVE RIGHT Beaded board is far cheaper than a tiled backsplash, especially when you consider the cost of installation. This beaded board is scored paneling instead of thicker and costlier individual boards. If you want to change your color scheme, it's easy to repaint.

Create the look/Fabric fixes

1. A livable kitchen offers charm and conceals some of the functional details. A washable skirt made from vintage linen sheets covers the island and hides clutter; it's attached using hook-and-loop fastening tape. The island is on casters so it can scoot to one side of the room during parties.

Fabric Fixes

Fabric has a softening effect on any space and helps give a kitchen a livable feel. A yard of fabric can skirt a sink or make a valance; multiple yards can dress up an island or drape a window from ceiling to floor. Before you start shopping, consider these tips.

- CHOOSE WASHABLE FABRICS FOR THE KITCHEN. FABRICS TREATED FOR SOIL AND STAIN RESISTANCE ARE SMART CHOICES.

- LOOK FOR READY-MADE CURTAINS THAT CAN BE EMBELLISHED TO SUIT YOUR SPACE. FUSIBLE WEBBING AND FABRIC GLUE MAKE IT EASY TO ADD RIBBONS AND FRINGE.

- TABLECLOTHS, NAPKINS, AND TEA TOWELS OFFER YARDAGE THAT CAN BE MADE INTO CURTAINS, SLIPCOVERS, AND MORE.

- SELECT FABRIC TO FIT THE STYLE OF THE ROOM. COTTON IS WASHABLE AND CASUAL. TOILE DRESSES UP THE ROOM; STRIPES RELAX THE MOOD.

- CONSIDER INDOOR/OUTDOOR FABRICS. THEY'RE A GOOD CHOICE BECAUSE THEY SHED MOISTURE AND STAINS.

2 If there's room in your kitchen, consider adding soft seating. A slipcovered chair feels right at home snuggled up to the kitchen desk and provides a comfy spot for planning meals and paying bills.

3 Give your drop-in sink the illusion of an apron-front model: Remove the base cabinet doors, replace them with a skirt gathered on a tension rod, and fit the rod to the cabinet frame. Use washable fabric for easy care.

4 Keep your windows wide open and sunny with a narrow valance that skims the window top with color and pattern. Checked tabs add a fun detail.

5 Here's a quick, budget-smart makeover: Remove recessed cabinet panels and replace them with chicken wire and fabric, stapled in place. Fabric panels could also be gathered on rods mounted to the inside of the cabinet door.

small SPACES

CHAPTER
6

It can be a tight fit to cook, eat, and congregate in a small kitchen. Discover ways to shoehorn storage into unexpected corners and visually expand the space with neutrals and open cabinetry. Then add big personality with color.

COMPACT CHARACTER

A traditional kitchen can be small and still make a design statement. A **SMART USE OF COLOR AND SPACE** produces a kitchen that works as well as, or better than, an oversize one. Consider this: A small kitchen requires fewer steps between workstations, demands a **WELL-EDITED SUPPLY OF KITCHEN GEAR,** and relies on a few key countertop accessories—all advantages for an efficient and tiny space.

OPPOSITE Opt for simplicity when refreshing a small kitchen. Basic door panels painted white anchor the look. White and gray countertops blend with the stainless-steel appliances. The floor picks up the same neutral tones. Even the tailored rattan shade blends in.

RIGHT An oversize checked floor pattern, placed on the diagonal, stretches apparent room size. Extra-tall cabinets, at 42 inches rather than 36 inches, offer bonus storage. A narrow island slides in to add counter and storage space along with a dining ledge. Purchase scaled-down appliances that lend style.

BARGAIN BONUS: STRETCH THE IMPACT OF EXPENSIVE MATERIALS BY PAIRING A SMALL AMOUNT, SUCH AS A PIECE OF MARBLE BACKSPLASH, WITH PAINTED WALLS.

Shelves open to view **OFFER BOTH STYLE AND STORAGE.** Limit how many items you store on open shelves and in glass-door cabinets, or the kitchen will feel cluttered.

◄ **LEFT** Doors with glass inserts and glass shelves give the room an open feel and also make storage look bigger. For an easy and inexpensive option, consider removing doors and painting cabinet interiors.

► **OPPOSITE** A neutral color scheme sets the tone for a small kitchen that looks big. Dark or bright colors can make a small kitchen feel claustrophobic. Matching countertop and island materials maintains a good visual flow.

BARGAIN BONUS:
LOOK FOR AFFORDABLE,
OFF-THE-RACK RATTAN
BLINDS AND SHADES THAT
CAN BE TRIMMED TO FIT
OR HUNG OUTSIDE A
WINDOW FRAME WITHOUT
TRIMMING.

PRICED-RIGHT WHITE

When it comes to saving money, **WHITE IS AN AFFORDABLE OPTION.** After all, white cabinets, white flooring, and white countertops can be **PICKED UP IN STOCK FOR BIG SAVINGS.** Incorporating lots of white can make a space feel airy if not downright roomy.

OPPOSITE Like the soft painted finish on the cabinets and window frames, matte ceramic-tile countertops reduce the chill factor in an all-white kitchen. Tiny cream-color squares set into the tiled backsplash keep a monochromatic palette from being uninteresting. Roman-style rattan shades and a checkerboard floor of taupe and white also increase visual interest.

RIGHT Painted white like the other cabinets, the faux hutch features low-cost lumberyard add-ons: beaded-board plywood for the backsplash, wood molding for the countertop edge, and shapely wood shelf brackets for "feet." Center panels on the solid-panel doors create visual depth.

BARGAIN BONUS: VINYL TILE SQUARES LOOK GREAT IN CHECKERBOARD PATTERNS. LOOK FOR SELF-ADHESIVE VERSIONS FOR EASY INSTALLATION.

Create the look/White cabinets

1. Painting cabinets white updates a tired look, but the process can be time-consuming. If you want color, spread it on the walls. When you decide to change the color scheme, it's much easier to repaint the walls than the cabinets.

The Right White?

White is a perennial color favorite, especially for kitchens. It feels clean, bright, and timeless. It's also a smart option when affordability is paramount. Here are some tips to help make white right.

- MIX WARM AND COOL WHITES TO STABILIZE VISUAL TEMPERATURES. TRY THIS EXPERIMENT: GATHER A COLLECTION OF SHELLS ON A PLATTER. LOOK CLOSELY. YOU'LL SEE TAN, PINK, YELLOW, AND BLUE TINTING THE WHITES. THAT SAME VARIETY SHOULD BE PRESENT IN ANY WHITE ROOM.

- CHOOSE A BASE OF WARM WHITE IF THE KITCHEN FACES NORTH OR EAST, A COOL ONE IF IT'S ORIENTED SOUTH OR WEST.

- CONSIDER NATURAL AND ARTIFICIAL LIGHT. A TOO-BRIGHT WHITE CAN MAKE YOUR KITCHEN FEEL LIKE THE INSIDE OF THE REFRIGERATOR WITH THE LIGHT ON.

- BRING IN FABRIC AND PAINT SWATCHES TO SEE HOW THE WHITES CHANGE FROM DAWN TO DARK. THAT'S THE BEST GUARANTEE YOU'LL PICK THE RIGHT WHITE.

- PLAY SHINY AGAINST MATTE TO ADD INTEREST. VARY PAINT SHEENS FROM HIGH-GLOSS TO MATTE, AND FABRICS FROM POLISHED COTTON TO NUBBY LINEN.

2 Black provides a grounding note to an all-white scheme. Use the contrast to create visual interest, such as this backsplash covered with black-and-white prints framed and hung as art.

3 When cabinets cramp a kitchen, remove as many upper cabinets as possible; then treat the remainder to a space-expanding coat of white paint.

4 A distressed white finish gives these cabinets a warm look that reflects the natural tones of the wood ceiling. White can be dressy in a glossy finish or rustic when woodtones show through.

5 Warm woods and cool whites make great kitchen companions. Painting a wall of cabinetry in white turns it into a backdrop that simply disappears.

FRENCH FOREVER

A typical U-shape kitchen might be short on space, but it **SHOULD ALWAYS HAVE ROOM FOR STYLE.** In this kitchen redo, rich red and gold give the room a decidedly French accent. Bold toile wallpaper adds a dressy note that **MAKES THE KITCHEN CHARMING RATHER THAN UTILITARIAN,** a fun way to blur the lines when cooking and dining occupy the same space.

BARGAIN BONUS: WHITE APPLIANCES PROVIDE THE SAME FUNCTION AS MORE EXPENSIVE STAINLESS-STEEL UNITS.

OPPOSITE Sunflower yellow cabinets at eye level help lighten the room, while deep red base cabinets have a grounding effect. The two combine to make the small space feel warm and cozy.

ABOVE LEFT Cabinet doors and drawers distressed by hand offer the room an aged elegance that is practical, affordable, and in keeping with French style. Paint can extend the life of dated cabinets and save thousands of dollars.

ABOVE RIGHT Painting the wood countertop edging adds a spark of color. Gather accessories that spread the color scheme around the space.

PAINT FOR STYLE

When a dated kitchen is crying out for a makeover and your budget says halt, **PAINT IS YOUR BEST DECORATING FRIEND.** In this compact kitchen, paint updated the countertops, cabinets, vinyl flooring, and kitchen gear. Paint even added a pop of color to off-the-rack roller shades.

BARGAIN BONUS: always test paint products in a hidden area. It's crucial to know whether a primer or paint will stick to the surface.

OPPOSITE A color palette of gray, cream, and shiny stainless steel makes this small kitchen seem huge. Too much color and pattern might call attention to flaws rather than hiding them.

ABOVE Dated laminate countertops, once bright red, hide under a coat of charcoal paint. Shop your paint store for durable paints and primers. The stripes on the cake stand were added using paint for glass, available at crafts stores.

BARGAIN BONUS: use a single roll of wallpaper to add pattern and color to a backsplash for a bargain price.

CRAFT A JEWEL

A SKINNY GALLEY KITCHEN offers one bonus to the budget: It's so small that it's easier to KEEP COSTS UNDER CONTROL. Use the savings for a splurge, such as pretty tile or an elegant faucet.

OPPOSITE Paint is the magic and affordable makeover material used to freshen dated oak cabinets. Black paint on the bottom cabinets and creamy white on the tops is a classic color combination. The color splurge? Aqua in countertops and stained glass for cabinet doors.

ABOVE An antique sink that cost just $25 creates the perfect attitude for this small kitchen. Install it like any countertop-mounted sink.

TOP RIGHT Wood feet added to cabinet bases create the look of custom cabinetry. Paint the feet to match the cabinets. Check the toe-kick space for fit. For sources for cabinet feet, see page 143.

BOTTOM RIGHT Adding pretty glass knobs and replacing false cabinet fronts with perforated metal panels updates the sink cabinet. The metal panels can be cut using tin snips and held in place with brads.

Bargain Bonus: Plain white tiles offer an affordable and classic option for kitchen walls. Look for them at a home center.

INCH BY INCH

A kitchen **SHORT ON SPACE** still has to function for cooking, cleanup, eating, and socializing. Here's how to make it work. **CABINETS CREATE A STORAGE WALL** and window seats for dining, **CUSTOM TOUCHES** make the working side of the kitchen look like a vintage cabinet, and **TWIN TABLES MOVE WHERE NEEDED**.

OPPOSITE Smaller than many pantries, this dressy kitchen organizes the workflow. Narrow slices of countertop measure just 24 inches on each side of the sink. Work areas are supplemented by matching bistro tables. Spices line the shelf behind the generous farm sink.

ABOVE Two small tables multiply the versatility of a tiny dining room and give it a bistro attitude. The built-in cabinets offer needed storage space for kitchen gear, window seats for dining, and bulkheads for hiding recessed lighting. Lift-up bench tops provide storage for oversize kitchen equipment.

TOP RIGHT What looks like a cabinet next to the sink is a cover-up for the dishwasher. Custom-made iron pins eliminate the need for door pulls, which would clutter the cabinet. Note that the cabinet door folds out of the way for loading or unloading of the dishwasher.

BOTTOM RIGHT Open storage surrounds the refrigerator and gracefully stores platters and wine bottles. The cubbies keep everything appointed in its place—a crucial strategy in a small kitchen.

Create the look/Space savers

(1) A table and trunk combination provides closed storage for big items and
display space for stacking bowls. Pull up a chair, and the table works for dining.
Multiuse pieces like this ensure efficient use of a small area.

Clever Strategies

Saving space demands the mindset of an engineer, the craftiness of a shipbuilder, and the style of a decorator. Here are some ideas to try.

- CLEAR CLUTTER. IT'S THE FIRST STEP IN DESIGNING SMALL KITCHENS.

- EMBRACE THE LIGHT. WHITE PAINT AND FABRICS, MINIMAL WINDOW TREATMENTS, AND SHINY SURFACES SPREAD SUNSHINE AROUND AND KEEP A SMALL SPACE FROM FEELING CLAUSTROPHOBIC.

- CONSIDER ADAPTABLE STORAGE. LOOK FOR AREAS TO ADD NARROW SHELVES, SUCH AS AT THE END OF AN ISLAND OR NEAR A BACKSPLASH. INCORPORATE BASKETS AND BOXES THAT CAN BE STACKED AND MOVED WHEREVER YOU NEED THEM. USE HOOKS UNDER A WINDOW OR ALONG A WALKWAY TO HOLD APRONS, TOWELS, AND OTHER KITCHEN ITEMS.

- LIMIT PATTERN. TOO MUCH PATTERN CAN MAKE A ROOM FEEL FRANTIC. FOR A CALMING EFFECT USE TEXTURE INSTEAD OF PATTERN TO ADD INTEREST.

- ADD A MIRROR OR TWO. MIRRORS EXPAND LIGHT AND VIEWS AND ADD IMMEDIATE STYLE. USE THEM NEAR A DINING AREA OR ABOVE THE COUNTERTOP.

2 A narrow counter tucked under a window can change how a kitchen works. It provides a landing spot by the back door and functions equally well as a spot to prepare or eat a meal. Never underestimate the power of inches to change the way a room functions.

3 Extra storage can be found in almost any nook or cranny. A bench snuggled up to a wall provides bonus space. Top the bench with comfortable cushions. Built-in cabinets along one end of the room look almost like a paneled wall.

4 Glass doors and shiny materials illustrate two space-saving strategies: See-through spaces multiply visual impact, while reflective materials expand light. Other strategies include leaving windows open to outside views and painting cabinets or ceilings with high-gloss paint.

5 In a small kitchen, crucial extra space is often defined by inches rather than feet. That's why adding storage room at the end of an island is so effective.

Index

Sources

p. 10, p. 137
Cabinet feet—
• Classic Designs by Matthew Burak; tablelegs.com; 800/843-7405
• Rockler Woodworking and Hardware; rockler.com; 800/279-4441
• Van Dyke's Restorers; vandykes.com; 800/558-1234

p. 33
Stainless paint—Thomas' Liquid Stainless Steel; liquidstainlesssteel.com; 800/650-5699

p. 105
Discount fabric sources—
• Discount Fabrics USA; discountfabricusacorp.com; 977/271-2266
• Fabric Guru; fabricguru.com; 877/722-4878
• Lewis & Sheron Textile Co.; lsfabrics.com; 877/256-8448

p. 125
Primers—
• Fresh Start; Benjamin Moore; benjaminmoore.com
• XIM Primer; ximbonder.com